D for Drone

Different drones have slightly different features. However, there are quite many terms and elements that they share in common. If you know these common elements, it will be much easier for you to get started.

This book covers the relevant terminologies, with focus on elements that are common across most drone species.

They are written to be more human while being technically accurate and useful.

This book is not meant to be a model/brand specific tutorial.

<u>Restrictions on Alteration</u>

You may not modify the Book or create any derivative work of the Book or its accompanying documentation. Derivative works include but are not limited to translations.

   Copyright 2020 **Tomorrowskills.com**.

Table of Contents

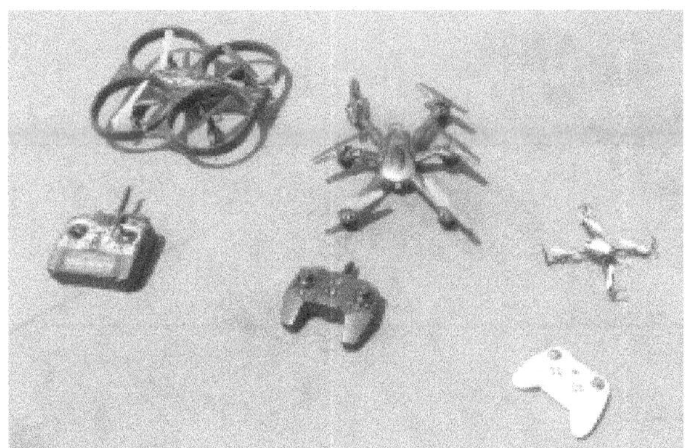

Drone and Quadchopper

RC means radio control. RC drones are hobbyist drones that can be remotely controlled via radio signals.

A drone is nothing more than an unmanned flying craft. Technically it is an unmanned aerial vehicle UAV. Unmanned means there is a pilot, but just that the pilot is not sitting inside the drone.

By definition a quadcopter may or may not be unmanned. It is simply a type of helicopter with four rotors.

Many consider a drone as a quadcopter since most drones run on 4 rotors as well.

Some RC drones have 6 rotors, which are easier to fly due to the extra stability introduced.

Rotors and Propellers

A rotor is like a fan (one that is motor driven and with spinning blades) serving as propellers pushing air down (in return, the air pushes up on the rotor).

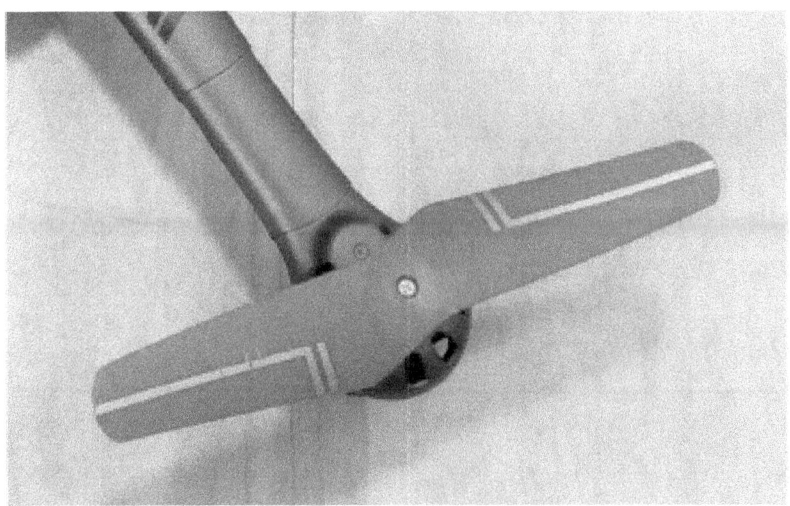

   Copyright 2020 **Tomorrowskills.com**.

Entry level drone propellers are always plastic. Higher end ones are carbon fiber. Very very few drones use metal propellers due to weight concern.

You should keep spare propellers because they are quite easy to go loose and eventually "disappear" upon crashing.

Most propellers do not require special installation procedure — you simply plug it back in. Of course, a little bit of glue may help secure it...

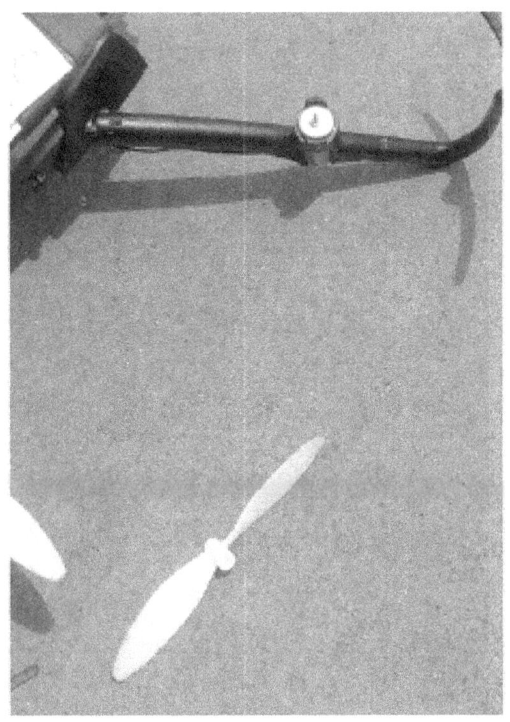

 Copyright 2020 **Tomorrowskills.com**.

The shape of the blades can make a performance difference but this is just not something you can easily change.

Some newer drone models have propellers with 3 or more blades.

FYI, propeller threads are always opposite to the motor spin direction so they won't get loose when flying.

Puller and pusher props

The propellers at the front of the drone are pullers that pull the drone through the air. Those at the rear end, in contrast, are pushers.

For maintaining a proper balance, propeller rotation is always toward the drone body. The front left one and the rear right one always go clockwise.

The front right one and the rear left one, in contrast, always go counter-clockwise. The rotation direction never changes. Only the speed changes per your request.

Some propellers are directly connected to the motor shaft, which is a low cost direct drive arrangement.

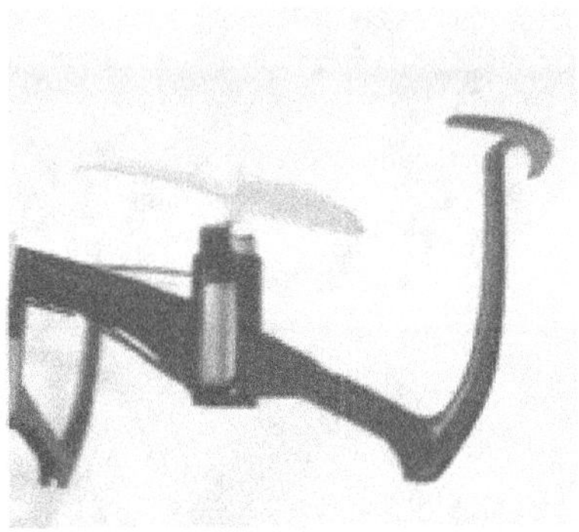

Advanced designs involve using gears —
typically a motor pinion gear and a spur
gear. This arrangement can increase motor
torque, which is necessary for supporting
larger propellers.

Vertical movement

As said before, when the propellers rotate
they effectively push down on the air, and
in return the air pushes up on the drone so
the   drone   can   fly   up   against   the

gravitational force.

The gravitational force always serves to pull down the drone, while movement is achieved by changing the rotation speed of certain rotors (or all rotors).

- When the down force roughly equals

the up force, the drone performs a hover still. It is hovering in the air in a rather stable manner. Very low end drones seldom hover well.

- When the down force is less than the up force (the propellers rotate faster), the drone is ascending.

- When the down force is stronger than the up force (the propellers rotate slower), the drone is descending.

 Copyright 2020 **Tomorrowskills.com**.

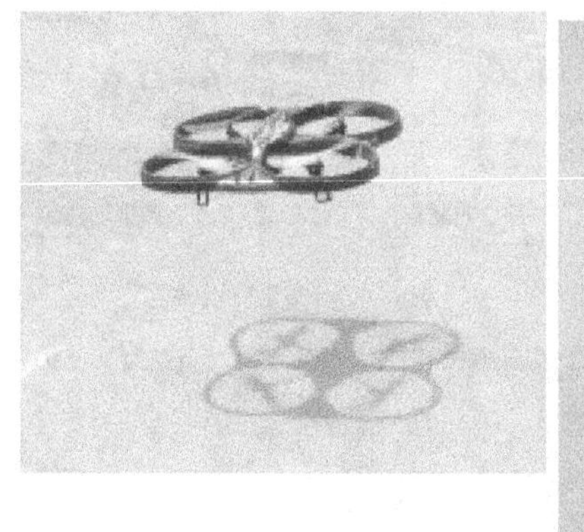 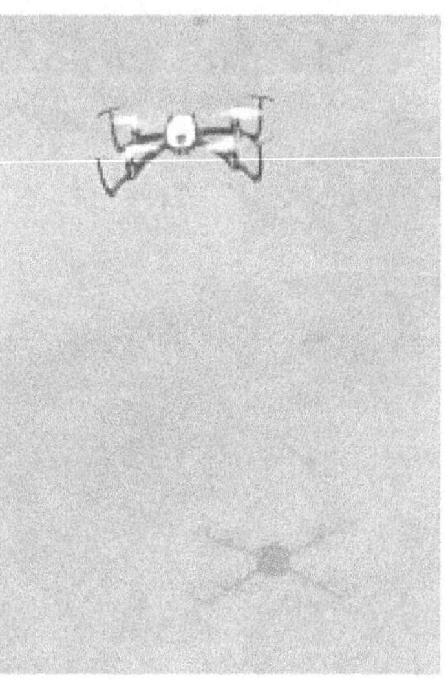

Proper hovering requires a very calm outdoor condition if your drone is small and lightweight. Very small drones are too small to stand against any wind and can hardly hover in a stable manner.

Horizontal movement

Horizontal movement is achieved differently.

- Roll means flying sideways (which involves leaning to the side).

- Yaw involves rotating the head of the drone to right or left so to spin the drone, all without leaning.

- Pitch means movement forward or

backward (leaning towards the front or the back).

Many drones are symmetrical (headless – there is no difference between front and rear) so the concept of moving forward and backward can become quite "vague".

Some drones are designed with the front propellers intentionally manufactured in a different color so you can easily spot the difference:

Often it is the viewing direction of the onboard camera or the led light of the drone that determines what is front and what is rear.

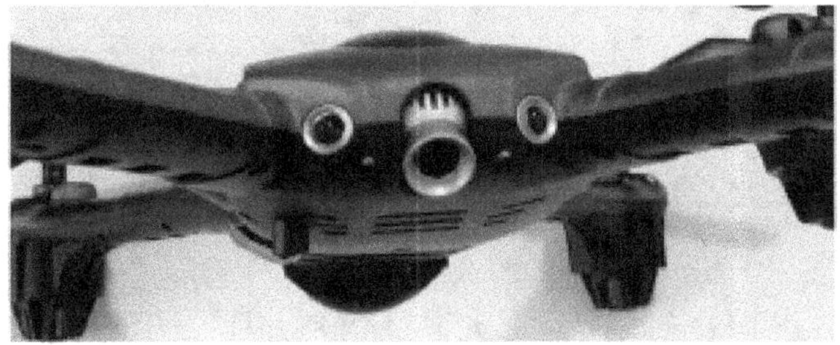

The sticks

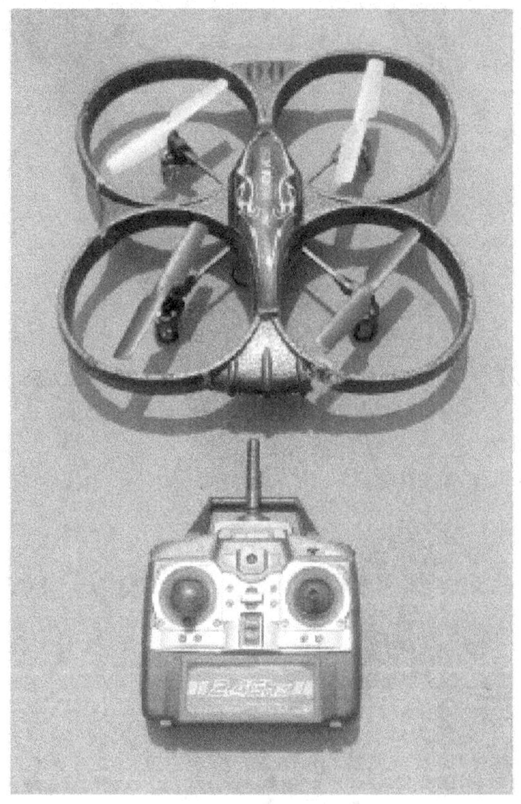

On the transmitter there is a left throttle
stick and also a right throttle stick. Unlike

 Copyright 2020 **Tomorrowskills.com**.

those for RC cars, these sticks can move 360 degree.

In reality, you need to use both together for proper flying. For simplicity sake, you want to know the basic operations of these sticks:

- you turn the left throttle stick either to the left or right in order to yaw (to rotate so to turn left or right without leaning).

- you move the left throttle stick forward and backward as needed to accelerate

 Copyright 2020 **Tomorrowskills.com**.

or decelerate (which is necessary to fly up/down and to pitch).

- you manipulate the right throttle stick so the drone can lean front & back or sideways.

   Copyright 2020 **Tomorrowskills.com**.

Carefree mode

Traditionally, when your drone has rotated with its front pointing towards yourself, a left on the transmitter will actually fly the it to the right. Similar problem with forward and backward – you push the stick forward and the drone will come back to you. This can become confusing.

In careless mode AKA headless mode, the drone will fly relative to your position no matter which way its frontend (or head) is

facing - it is just like there is no head at all .

Many newer drones support this mode.

Brushless

Motors used by modern drones are all brushless, which are small, lightweight, maintenance free and super powerful when comparing to the traditional motors.

Without brushless motors there is no way for RC drones to be achievable and practical.

Brushless motors ENABLE modern drones.

 Copyright 2020 **Tomorrowskills.com**.

Poor quality motors can cause vibration which makes it hard to keep the drone steady. Brushed motors can cause spark which can interfere with the radio. Fortunately, most brushless motors do not have these problems.

Higher end drones come with brushless motors labeled with their KV ratings. For beginners all you need to know is that higher KV rating means higher speed.

 Copyright 2020 **Tomorrowskills.com**.

High KV rating motors with smaller propellers (those that are shorter or with a smaller dimension) can produce very high speed and more power consumption.

Low KV rating motors with larger propellers can produce very stable flying experience and reasonable power consumption.

 Copyright 2020 **Tomorrowskills.com**.

RPM

Rotation per minute RPM is a measure that tells how fast the motor can run. Higher RPM means higher performance and more power hungry the motors are.

The weight of the drone as well as the weight of the propellers directly determine the actual workload (there are other factors, such as wind and altitute).

Lipo

Lipo batteries are rechargeable batteries that are small, lightweight and un-proportionately powerful when comparing to the traditional rechargeable batteries.

The voltage per cell is 3.7V (we refer to it as

one cell or 1S). Very small RC drones are usually running on this voltage, and the battery can be charged via very simple USB solution:

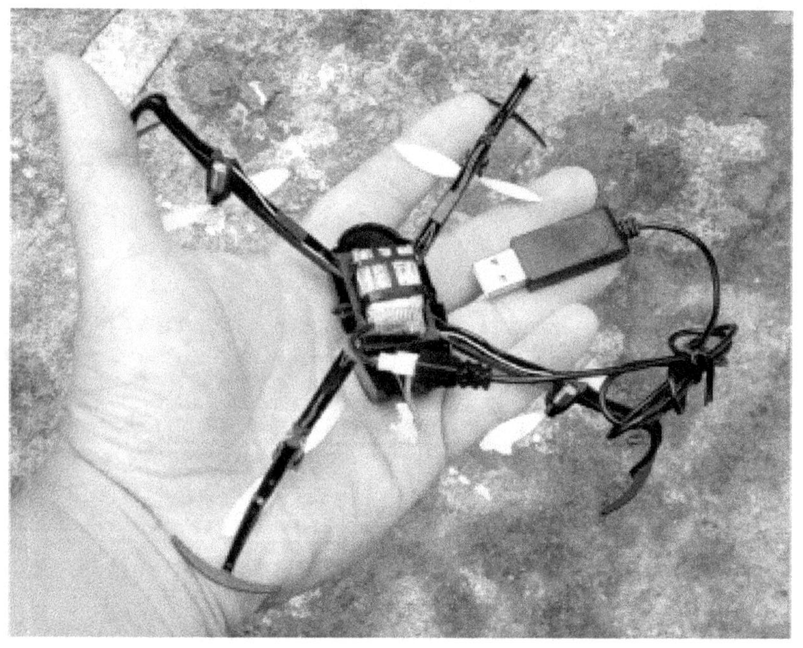

More powerful drones are based on 3.7V x 2

  Copyright 2020 **Tomorrowskills.com**.

(we call it 2 cells or 2s), 3.7V x 3 (3 cells or 3s) or even 3.7V x 4 (4 cells or 4s). These cannot be charged via USB since USB can hardly go over 5.5V.

Refer to the picture above, even a 2 cell

battery can be very small. It fits perfectly

well in the middle of the drone body.

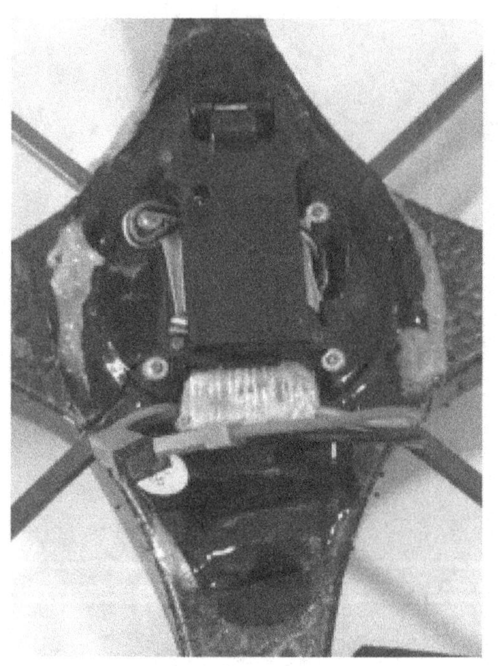

Together with brushless technology, Lipo

batteries ENABLE modern drones.

Keywords: small and powerful.

Lipo cells are not maintenance free though.

For them to survive you must keep them at

the proper voltage level at all time. Do not

overrun them. And do not over charge

them! Use smart charger or specialized

charging circuitry whenever possible!

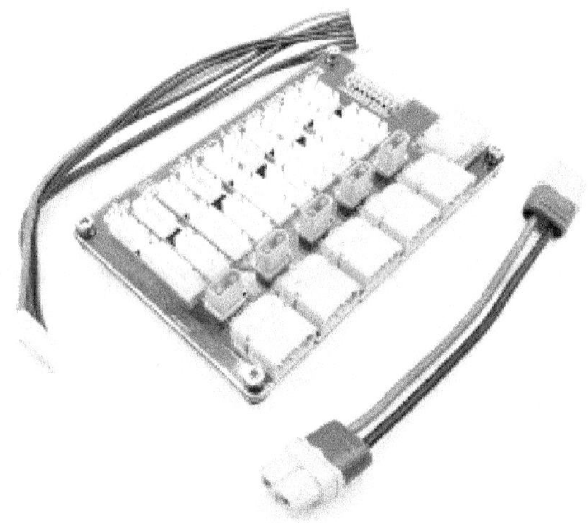

    Copyright 2020 **Tomorrowskills.com**.

Mah

The mah value of the battery determines your flight time. Larger mah means larger battery capacity.

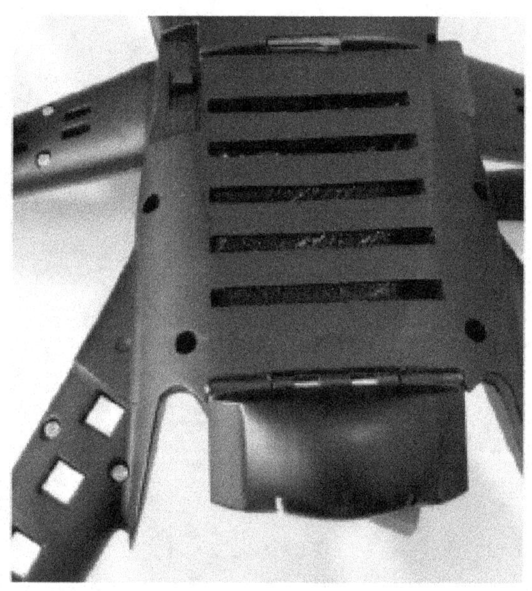

The thing is, the battery compartment of a

RC drone is usually small and tight.

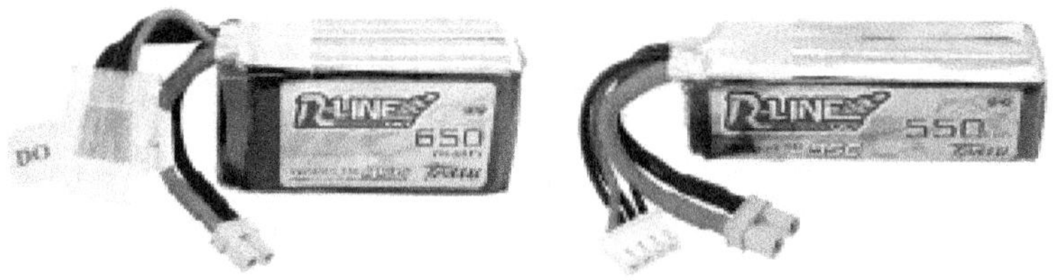

High capacity battery packs are usually

"thicker". You just cannot expect to have

very large capacity on a physically small and

thin battery.

Balanced charging

When your lipo battery is one cell only, there is no need for balance charging. When the battery has a very small capacity, balance charging may not always be required as well (since the risk is low).

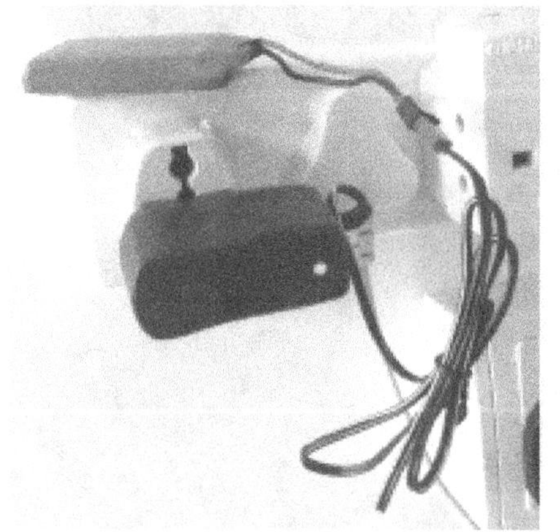

When it has more than one cells, balanced charging ensures every cell receive approximately the same amount of charge.

The picture below shows a battery with a separate charge lead for balancing charging.

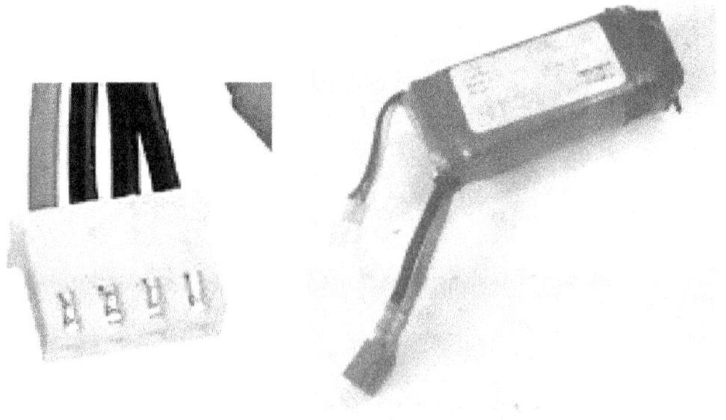

Modern lipo chargers are almost always capable of doing this. Some better ones even allow you to charge batteries for storage purpose.

Generally speaking, you should fly your drone with a fully charged battery within several days. Keeping a lipo battery fully charged for too long can be harmful to the battery! If your battery is to remain unused for a long period of time, use the charger's storage charge mode so the battery can receive the proper charge prior to storage.

JST connector

Drones that run on smaller 2-cell lipo batteries are usually equipped with JST connectors (usually red in color) for the battery connection.

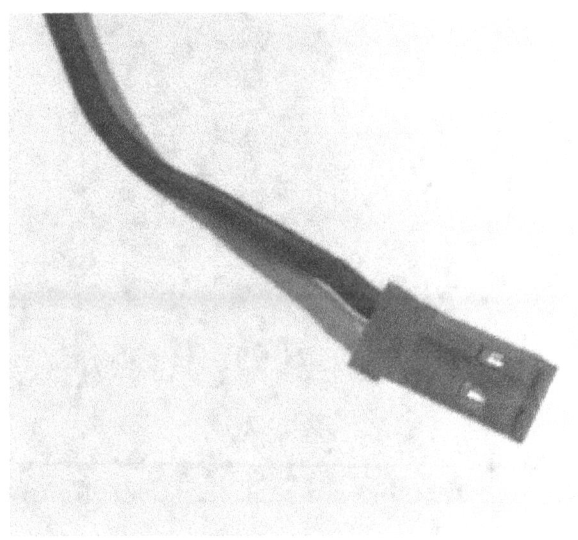

The above example shows the battery's male JST connector. The drone side has a female connector.

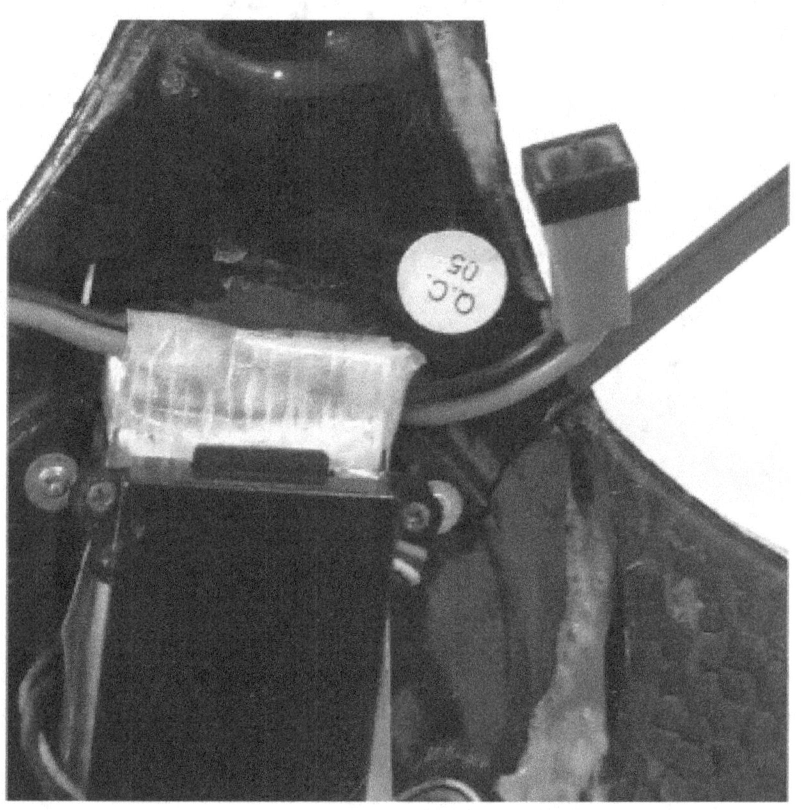

Entry level drones that run on 3.7V power often use Micro JST connectors, which are even smaller than the regular JST connectors. They are usually white in color.

Dean and XT60 connectors

Larger capacity lipo packs often use T connectors (aka Dean connectors). T connectors are very common in RC cars and boats. Note that the battery side always has the female connector.

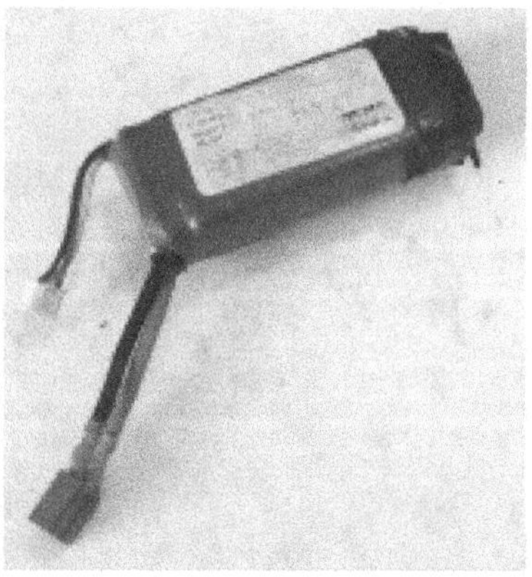

JST connectors are too weak to withstand

heat brought by stronger batteries. The wires that go with the JST connectors are also too thin — they can get real hot easily.

There are other connectors that can sustain high power. For example, XT60 and EC3. XT60 connectors are mostly yellow in color:

Radio control

Stick type transmitters are the most popular. Entry level transmitter often resembles the look of TV game joypad (and with sticks added to it).

 Copyright 2020 **Tomorrowskills.com**.

When you manipulate the remote control sticks on the transmitter, the transmitter will send signals to the drone's receiver (some call it the Flight Controller), which will in turn relay the information to the ESC Electronic Speed Controller.

The ESC will, accordingly, direct the motors to rotate (and supply the necessary power taken from the battery to the motors). Some ESC can support 4 motors, while some can support 6.

 Copyright 2020 **Tomorrowskills.com**.

Some models have an integrated circuit

board with the receiver and the ESC built

into one unit.

Radio frequency

Low end remote controllers work primarily using the 2.4 GHz frequency for controlling the drone. Higher end products can switch between this frequency and 5.8 GHz.

2.4 GHz is slower but has a longer range.

5.8 gives the exact opposite.

FYI, 2.4 GHz is the dominant radio frequency in use by the hobby industry nowadays. The controller can match with the receiver on the drone automatically. There is also no need for a long antenna on both sides.

Radio interference

When there are multiple drones in the same area, your 2.4G radio system should be able to make the necessary settings to avoid jamming.

HOWEVER, disruption is definitely possible when you are too close to sources like strong magnets, power lines, and cell towers.

LOS vs FOV

Maintaining Line of Sight LOS means that in any area in which your visual view of the surrounding airspace in which your drone operates must not be obscured by any obstacles or meteorological weather conditions.

It represents a straight line along which you have a clear view on the drone and the airspace around it.

From a starter perspective, this is "naturally required". What is the point of flying a drone when you cannot see it?

From a more tech oriented perspective, LOS may also be maintained with the help of visual devices, lenses, or even a third person observer (one who can communicate with you consistently)!

Field of view FOV is a totally different concept — it is the viewing angle from the drone's camera.

Maintaining FOV and maintaining LOS are two different things that are totally unrelated!

Technically, having FOV does not imply that you have proper LOS.

Camera and gimbal

A gimbal is sort of a support system that stabilizes your drone's camera. It allows the camera to rotate smoothly along an axis. On an advanced drone a proper gimbal would be implemented for 3- axis camera stabilization and anti-vibration.

The camera on a low end drone would not have any real gimbal but a cheap anti vibration mount (rubber buffered mounting).

On higher end drone there would be a real gimbal and also a camera control circuitry.

Advanced camera system allows the drone

to transmit whatever captured back to you

in real time. Lower end system simply offers

a slot for MicroSD card.

FPV

Shorts for First Person View, it refers to a ground level view of what the drone's camera can see and transmit back to you.

Some drone packages have dedicated LCD screens built into the transmitter, while some allows you to see things via your mobile phone.

 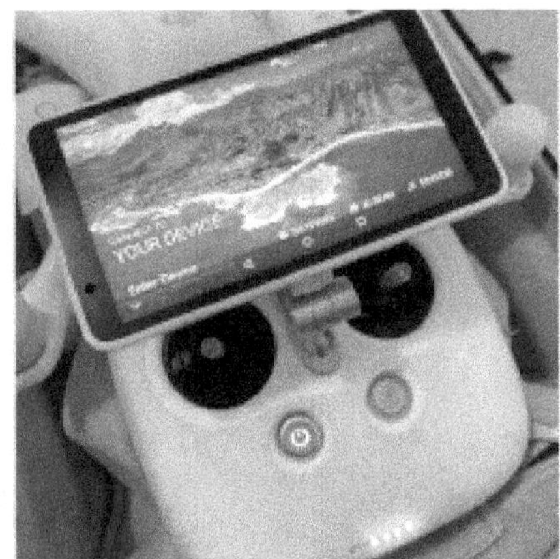

Real time system may be implemented using 2.4G radio or 5.8G radio. To avoid interfering with your drone's flying radio control frequency, 5.8G FPV is preferred.

Special 5.8G FPV antenna is usually

recommended for this to properly work.

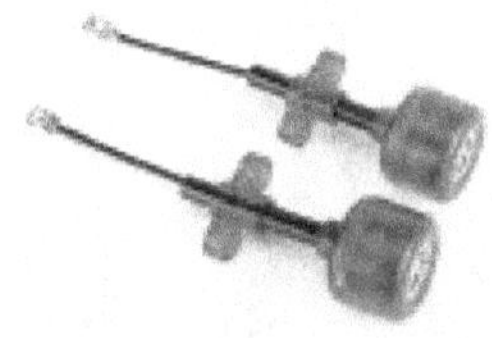

A complete headset with goggle is expensive

but is fun to use. It gives you FPV in real

time like a real pilot.

GPS

Global Positioning System GPS uses satellites

to provide location and time information to

the drone as long as there is an

unobstructed line of sight between the drone

and the GPS satellites.

Low end drones are NOT GPS capable. However, as long as you have a LOS, you do NOT need a GPS to fly a drone.

GPS is a US standard. Glonass is the Russian equivalence. Some advanced drones have support for either one of them or both.

Failsafe homing

Failsafe home point is an advanced feature which allows your drone to fly back when its connection with your transmitter is cut off for whatever reasons. GPS support is required to achieve this.

Landing gears

Drones that carry a high quality camera or a high capacity battery require high ground clearance. Usually there are skids attached directly to the bottom of the body or the motor mounts to serve as the landing gears.

Most landing gears are fixed. Only very high

end drones have retractable landing gears.

Protective land gears offer protection of the propellers in case your drone flips and eventually lands upside down.

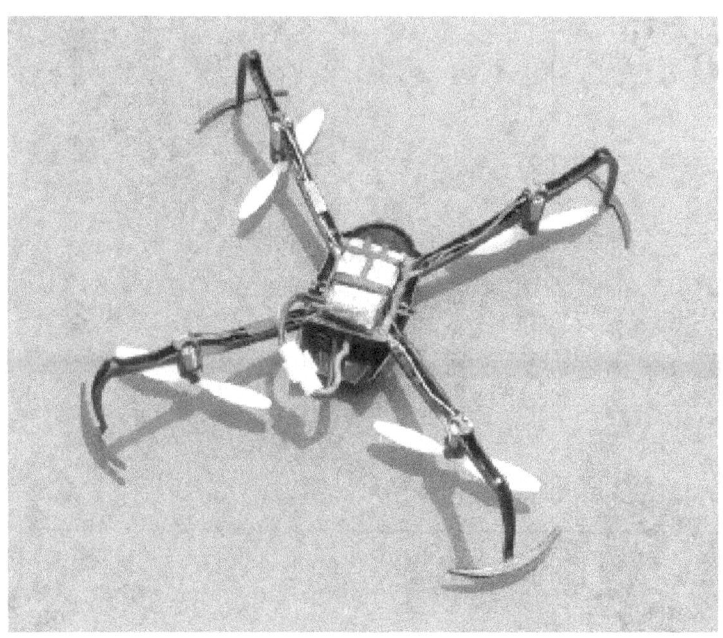

    Copyright 2020 **Tomorrowskills.com**.

Sensors

Different kinds of sensors are at work inside an advanced drone.

There are accelerometers that determine the position and orientation of your flying drone. There are tilt sensors that detect when the drone is to lean or incline. And there are gyroscopes that sense any deviation from the current flight path or any changes in orientation (i.e. detects and measures rotational motion).

There are some other sensors. And they are all connected to a small CPU inside your drone (modern day drones are all equipped with an onboard mini computer that are programmable).

As previously said, modern day drones are all equipped with an onboard mini computer. There is a chip that stores basic instructions for the CPU to follow, and we call it the firmware.

Advanced drones usually provide an interface for you to regularly update this firmware. You can download an update from the manufacturer's site and apply it to the firmware via model specific USB link.

Program your drone

Some drones allow you to program it. There is an onboard microcontroller so you can write program to automate its operation.

For starters, the DJI Tello allows kids to learn programming using Scratch code blocks on a regular Windows desktop or web browser.

If you visit Scratch's official site (https://scratch.mit.edu/) you should be able to find a lot of Tello projects that are open to everyone.

   Copyright 2020 **Tomorrowskills.com**.

Drone racers

Racers belong to a slightly different breed. They do not take photos or videos. They race!

Instead of allowing you to move up and down freely, there is a pair of ultrasonic sensors at the bottom of the frame which senses the distance with the ground so the onboard controller can maintain the altitude at a predetermined height (35cm or 60cm for the Kyosho Drone racers).

DJI, Phantom, Spark and Mavic

DJI is the dominant brand of drones in the market. From entry level drones to top of the line ones, DJI seems to be capable of offering the best possible quality.

Phantom, Spark and Mavic are DJI's most popular product lines.

In some regions DJI offers warranty policy to replace damaged drones with new ones.

 Copyright 2020 **Tomorrowskills.com**.

Parrot and PGYTECH

Parrot is another famous brand of drones.

Its Behop is a pretty popular entry level

drone.

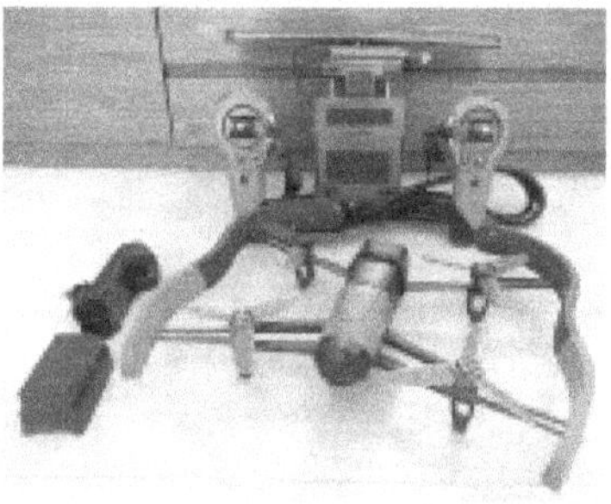

PGYTECH is another company which

produces high quality accessories for drone

photography.

Airframe

An airframe for drone is like a barebone kit — it has the frame and nothing else so you must acquire and assemble everything on your own.

Yuneec is a famous manufacturer with high quality fiber airframe products to offer.

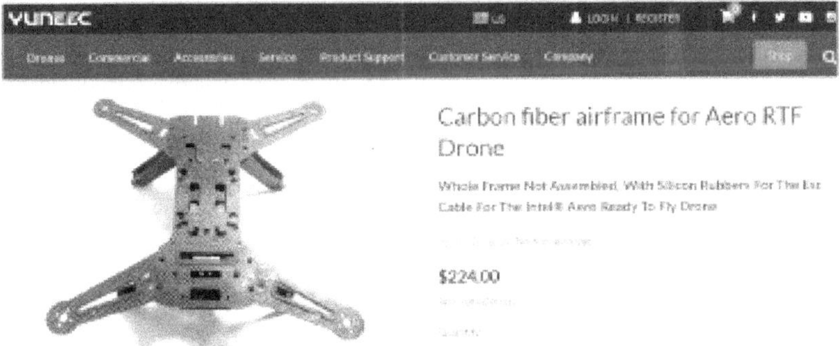

On the web you can also find many lower end airframe kits.

Putting together a drone is no easy task. You should consider doing it only if professional help is handy.

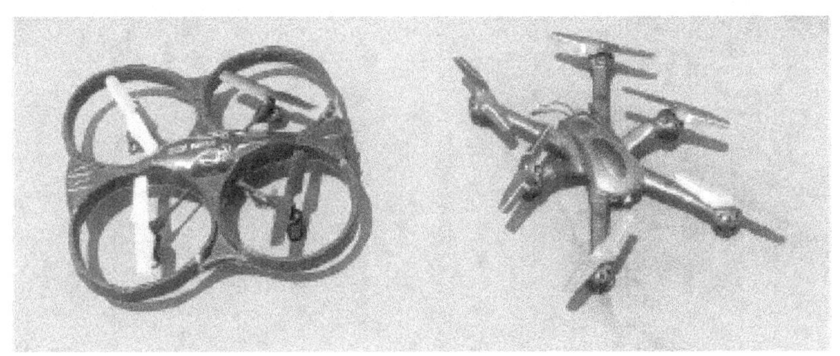

END OF BOOK

Please email your questions and comments

to admin@Tomorrowskills.com.

www.ingramcontent.com/pod-product-compliance
Lightning Source LLC
Chambersburg PA
CBHW071235240726
48654CB00009B/1056